Questions and Answers: Countries

El Salvador

A Question and Answer Book

by Kathleen W. Deady

Consultant:
Ralph Lee Woodward Jr.
Emeritus Professor of Latin American History
Tulane University
New Orleans, Louisiana

Capstone
press

Mankato, Minnesota

Fact Finders is published by Capstone Press,
151 Good Counsel Drive, P.O. Box 669, Mankato, Minnesota 56002.
www.capstonepress.com

Library of Congress Cataloging-in-Publication Data
Deady, Kathleen W.
El Salvador: A question and answer book / by Kathleen W. Deady.
    p. cm.—(Fact finders. Questions and answers. Countries)
    Includes bibliographical references and index.
    ISBN 0-7368-3750-7 (hardcover)
    1. El Salvador—Juvenile literature. I. Title. II. Series.
F1483.2.D43 2005
972.84—dc22   2004011357

Summary: Describes the geography, history, economy, and culture of El Salvador in a
    question-and-answer format.

Editorial Credits
Katy Kudela, editor; Kia Adams, set designer; Kate Opseth, book designer; Nancy Steers,
    map illustrator; Wanda Winch, photo researcher; Scott Thoms, photo editor

Photo Credits
Capstone Press, 29 (bill); Corbis/Reuters/Luis Galdamez, 15; Cory Langley, cover (both);
Getty Images Inc./Hulton Archive, 7; Getty Images Inc./AFP/Yuri Cortez, 9; One Mile Up
Inc., 29 (flag); Photo courtesy of Dan Drew, 29 (coins); Photo courtesy of Didier Martin, 12,
24; South American Pictures/Chris Sharp, 4, 11; South American Pictures/Jason P. Howe,
13, 17, 18–19, 21, 25, 27; South American Pictures/Robert Francis, 1; The Viesti Collection
Inc./Joe Viesti, 23

Artistic Effects
Ingram Publishing, 16; Photodisc/Jules Frazier, 18

1 2 3 4 5 6 10 09 08 07 06 05

Table of Contents

Features

Where is El Salvador?

El Salvador is the smallest country in Central America. It is slightly smaller than the U.S. state of Massachusetts.

El Salvador's land is varied. Mountains cover much of the land. A narrow strip of lowlands lies along the Pacific coast.

People call the volcano Izalco the Lighthouse of the Pacific. ➤

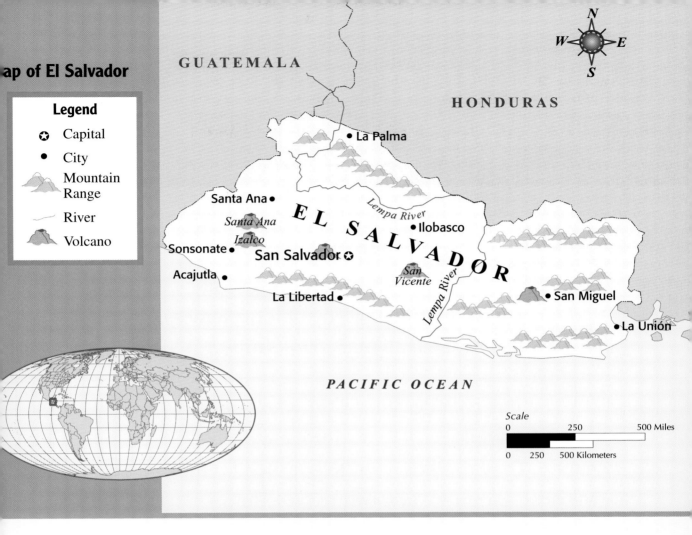

Legend

⊛ Capital
● City
⛰ Mountain Range
〜 River
🌋 Volcano

GUATEMALA

HONDURAS

● La Palma

Santa Ana ●

EL SALVADOR

Santa Ana
Izalco
Sonsonate ●
San Salvador ⊛

Lempa River
● Ilobasco

San Vicente
Lempa River

Acajutla ●

La Libertad ●

● San Miguel

● La Unión

PACIFIC OCEAN

Scale
0 — 250 — 500 Miles
0 — 250 — 500 Kilometers

El Salvador is often called the Land of Volcanoes. The country has several active volcanoes, such as Izalco and San Miguel. The tallest active volcano is Santa Ana. It stands 7,757 feet (2,364 meters) high.

When did El Salvador become a country?

El Salvador declared its **independence** on September 15, 1821. On this day, El Salvador and four other Central American **colonies** split from Spain. The other colonies were Costa Rica, Guatemala, Honduras, and Nicaragua.

The five colonies joined the Mexican Empire. People in El Salvador were not happy. They did not want to be ruled by the Mexican Empire. They wanted freedom.

Fact!

Spaniard Pedro de Alvarado and his army attacked El Salvador in 1524. He claimed the land for Spain. Spain ruled El Salvador for almost 300 years after the attack.

Manuel José Arce served as the first president of the United Provinces of Central America.

In 1823, El Salvador and the other four colonies broke from the Mexican Empire. They formed the United Provinces of Central America. In 1841, El Salvador split itself from this group. El Salvador created its own government.

What type of government does El Salvador have?

El Salvador's government is a **republic**. Like the United States, El Salvador has an executive and a legislative branch. El Salvador's government meets in San Salvador, the capital city.

A president and vice president head the executive branch. They make choices for the country based on the constitution, or the written laws. Salvadorans elect a president and a vice president for a term of five years.

Fact!

El Salvador has had 23 constitutions. The most recent one was adopted December 23, 1983.

In 2004, Elias Antonio Saca was elected president.

The legislative branch makes laws. El Salvador's Legislative Assembly has 84 members. People vote for these members every three years.

What kind of housing does El Salvador have?

People live in many different kinds of houses in El Salvador. Outside the cities, some people live in houses made of **adobe**. The poorest people build huts with tree branches covered with mud.

Where do people in El Salvador live?

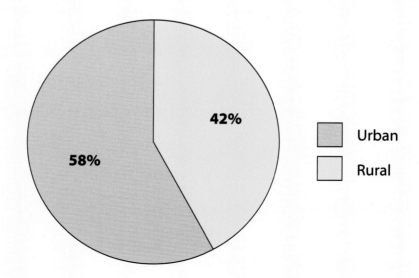

42%

58%

Urban

Rural

Some Salvadorans live in houses made of cardboard and tin.

In the cities, many people live in small tin or cardboard houses. Others live in apartments and small houses.

Rich Salvadorans own houses. Some of the rich live in or near the cities. Others live on large coffee **plantations** in the country.

What are El Salvador's forms of transportation?

Salvadorans have several ways to travel. People in towns and cities travel by bus. Many people also walk from place to place. In large cities, people can ride in taxis.

Visitors to El Salvador often arrive by plane. El Salvador has one international airport near San Salvador.

People use a cart and oxen on unpaved roads. ➤

People in large cities use taxis and buses to travel from place to place.

El Salvador has good city highways and roads. Roads outside the cities are often in poor shape. In the late 1970s, Salvadorans' fight for land and jobs led to a long **civil war**. The war damaged the country. Many roads have not been fixed since then.

What are El Salvador's major industries?

Farming is El Salvador's main **industry**. El Salvador's soil and climate are good for growing coffee beans. Farmers also grow cotton and sugarcane.

Many events have hurt El Salvador's businesses. Low coffee prices and civil war slowed growth in El Salvador. Natural disasters also damaged crops and buildings. Hurricane Mitch hit El Salvador in 1998. In 2001, El Salvador had a major earthquake.

What does El Salvador import and export?

Imports	Exports
electricity	coffee beans
food	sugar
petroleum	textiles

Workers on coffee plantations harvest the beans by hand.

El Salvador is working to add new businesses. Factories now make clothing and furniture. They also make rubber goods and medicines.

What is school like in El Salvador?

Schools in El Salvador are open from January through October. Children must go to school from ages 7 to 12. They can attend public schools for free.

Some Salvadoran families pay for their children to go to a private school. Religious groups run these schools.

Children in El Salvador study math, history, and geography. They also take computer classes and physical education classes.

Fact!

About one in every five adults in El Salvador cannot read or write.

Students go to school for 10 months of the year.

El Salvador does not have enough teachers or schools. Many children leave school to work. Others cannot afford school supplies. El Salvador is working hard to improve its public schools.

What are El Salvador's favorite sports and games?

Soccer is the favorite sport in El Salvador. Salvadorans enjoy watching school teams play soccer. They also watch local and pro teams. El Salvador's national team plays in the World Soccer League.

Salvadorans also play many other sports. Basketball and baseball are popular. Some people ride bikes and motorcycles. Other popular sports include horseback riding, tennis, and golf.

Fact!

Salvadorans call national soccer star Jorge Gonzalez the "Magician." He is known for his speed and skills.

Children play soccer on school teams.

People in El Salvador enjoy their free time. Many people get together to fish and go swimming. Children play games that are like hopscotch and marbles.

What are the traditional art forms in El Salvador?

Salvadorans make crafts from natural materials. People weave palm leaves into brooms and baskets. Some people use seeds and beads to make jewelry, such as necklaces and bracelets. They use wood to make toys and furniture.

Fact!

Colorful art fills the city of La Palma. The city's art came from Salvadoran artist Fernando Llort. He taught his art style to many young artists.

Artists in La Palma make colorful crafts.

Artists are found in many Salvadoran cities. Potters in Ilobasco are famous for their **ceramic** figures. Artists in La Palma are known for the colorful designs they paint on wood, ceramics, and jewelry.

What major holidays do people in El Salvador celebrate?

Many holidays in El Salvador are religious celebrations. The first week of August is the Feast of the Holy Savior, El Salvador's **patron saint**. People get together for parades, music, and food. Towns also hold festivals for their own patron saints.

Christmas is also a weeklong celebration in El Salvador. Families have nightly *posadas*, or parades. They go to church on Christmas Eve. Children receive gifts.

What other holidays do people in El Salvador celebrate?

Columbus Day
Labor Day
New Year's Day
Teacher's Day

Parades are part of many religious holidays.

September 15 is Independence Day.
People celebrate the day El Salvador became
free from Spain. Many people have time off
from work and school. They watch parades
and have family picnics.

What are the traditional foods of El Salvador?

Salvadorans cook traditional foods with corn, beans, and rice. They use corn flour to make flat, round bread called tortillas. Tortillas are folded and filled with stewed or fried beans called frijoles (free-HOH-lays). Cooks may add rice, vegetables, and meat.

Fact!

Street merchants in El Salvador sell pupusas. Pupusas are small cornmeal pancakes. They are filled with soft white cheese, refried beans, and fried pork rinds.

People can buy fresh fruits and vegetables at markets.

Tamales are corn dough wrapped and cooked in banana leaves. Tamales are often filled with meat.

Many foods are available to people in the cities. Markets sell fresh meats, fish, fruits, and vegetables.

What is family life like in El Salvador?

Family is the center of Salvadoran life. Most families are large with four or more children. Children and their parents may live with grandparents, aunts, and uncles.

Before El Salvador's civil war, women stayed home to care for the family. Men helped with farmwork and other jobs.

What are the ethnic backgrounds of people in El Salvador?

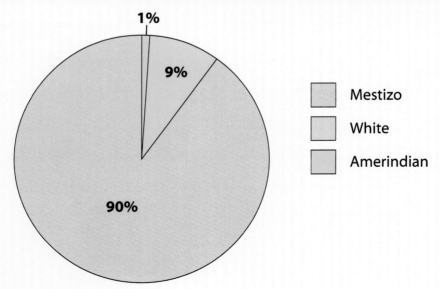

1%

9%

90%

Mestizo

White

Amerindian

Families in El Salvador sometimes tour city sites.

El Salvador's civil war weakened the country. It also hurt families. Now both parents often hold jobs. Many men cannot find work near home. They must leave their families to find work in other cities.

El Salvador Fast Facts

Official name:

Republic of El Salvador

Land area:

*8,000 square miles
(20,720 square kilometers)*

Average annual precipitation:

80 inches (203 centimeters)

Average January temperature (San Salvador):

*72 degrees Fahrenheit
(22 degrees Celsius)*

Average July temperature (San Salvador):

*73 degrees Fahrenheit
(23 degrees Celsius)*

Population:

6,587,541 people

Capital city:

San Salvador

Language:

Spanish

Natural resource:

farmable land

Religions:

Roman Catholic	*83%*
Other	*17%*

Money and Flag

Money:

Until 2001, El Salvador's money was the colón. In January 2001, El Salvador began using the U.S. dollar as well as the colón. The government hoped to bring world businesses to El Salvador. In 2004, 1 U.S. dollar equaled 8.75 colones. One Canadian dollar equaled 6.69 colones.

Flag:

The El Salvadoran flag has three stripes. The blue stripes stand for unity. The white stripe stands for peace. In the middle of the white stripe is the national coat of arms. The triangle on the coat of arms stands for equality. The five flags represent the original Central American nations.

Learn to Speak Spanish

People in El Salvador speak Spanish. It is El Salvador's official language. Learn to speak some Spanish using the words below.

English	Spanish	Pronunciation
yes	sí	(SEE)
no	no	(NOH)
hello	hola	(OH-lah)
good-bye	adiós	(ah-dee-OHS)
please	por favor	(POR fah-VOR)
thank you	gracias	(GRAH-see-us)
good morning	buenos días	(BWAY-nohs DEE-ahs)
good evening	buenas noches	(BWAY-nohs NO-chays)
How are you?	¿Cómo estás?	(KOH-moh ay-STAHS)

Glossary

adobe (uh-DOH-bee)—a building material made of clay mixed with straw and dried in the sun

ceramic (suh-RAM-ik)—having to do with objects made out of clay

civil war (SIV-il WOR)—war between groups of people in the same country

colony (KOL-uh-nee)—an area that is settled by people from another country and that is ruled by that country

independence (in-di-PEN-duhnss)—freedom from the control of other people or things

industry (IN-duh-stree)—a single branch of business or trade

patron saint (PAY-trun SAYNT)—a person honored by the Christian Church for leading a holy life

plantation (plan-TAY-shuhn)—a large farm that grows crops like coffee, tea, and cotton

republic (ree-PUHB-lik)—a government headed by a president with officials elected by the people

Internet Sites

FactHound offers a safe, fun way to find Internet sites related to this book. All of the sites on FactHound have been researched by our staff.

Here's how:
1. Visit *www.facthound.com*
2. Type in this special code **0736837507** for age-appropriate sites. Or enter a search word related to this book for a more general search.
3. Click on the **Fetch It** button.

FactHound will fetch the best sites for you!

Read More

Deady, Kathleen W. *El Salvador.* Countries of the World. Mankato, Minn.: Bridgestone Books, 2002.

Deem, James M. *El Salvador.* Top 10 Countries of Recent Immigrants. Berkeley Heights, N.J.: MyReportLinks.com Books, 2004.

Nickles, Greg. *El Salvador. The People and Culture.* The Lands, Peoples, and Cultures Series. New York: Crabtree, 2002.

Index